WARNING
POTATOES
HANDLE WITH CARE

D0713404

THE EYE SPY LOOKALIKE BOOK

PRIVATE EYE · ANDRE DEUTSCH

Private Eye Productions Ltd
6 Carlisle Street, London W1
in association with Andre Deutsch Ltd
105 Great Russell Street, London WC1.

© Pressdram Ltd 1988

ISBN 0 233 98335 X

Printed and bound in Great Britain
at The Bath Press, Avon

Lookalike

Kenneth Tynan

Larry Grayson

Sir,
    Seeing a picture of the late Kenneth Tynan I was struck by his resemblance to Mr Larry Grayson, the television personality.
    I wonder if by any chance they are related!

    ENA COURTAULD (Mrs), Whirlpool Farm, Etchingham, Sussex.

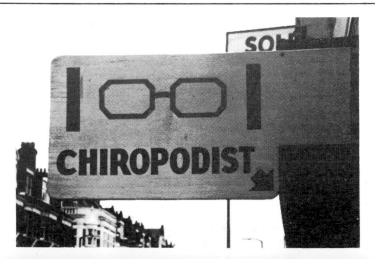

WARNING ALL DRIVERS
EXTREME CARE
BLIND PEOPLE
PATROLLING

BEWARE
SHEEP

Toilets · · No Diving

Lookalike

Marilyn Monroe   **Shirley Williams**

Sir,
I wonder if any of your readers has noticed the remarkable resemblance between Mrs Shirley Williams, the President of the SDP and Marilyn Monroe, the late Hollywood sex symbol.
I wonder if they are in any way related?

Yours faithfully,
MRS ENA POLLARD,
Wirral, Merseyside.

Lookalike

Prof. Margaret Gowing   **Peregrine Worsthorne**

Sir,
  I wonder whether any of your readers have noticed the resemblance between Professor Margaret Gowing, who is currently writing an official atomic history, and Mr Peregrine Worsthorne, editor of the Sunday Telegraph.
  I wonder if by any chance they are related?

  Yours,
  ENA B. HARTLEY.

Lookalike

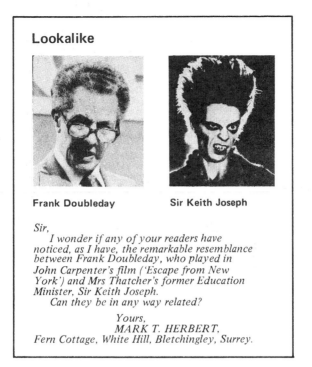

Frank Doubleday   **Sir Keith Joseph**

Sir,
 *I wonder if any of your readers have
noticed, as I have, the remarkable resemblance
between Frank Doubleday, who played in
John Carpenter's film ('Escape from New
York') and Mrs Thatcher's former Education
Minister, Sir Keith Joseph.*
 Can they be in any way related?

   Yours,
   MARK T. HERBERT,
Fern Cottage, White Hill, Bletchingley, Surrey.

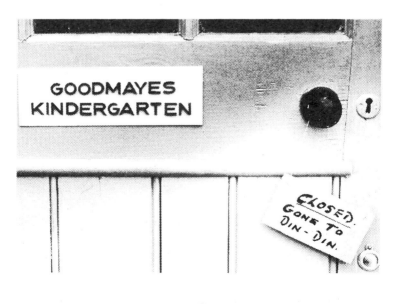

PLEASE: NO EXPLANATIONS INSIDE THE CHURCH.

Lookalike

Gleave

Waugh

Sir,
I wonder if any of your readers have noticed the resemblance between former *Private* Eye columnist *Auberon Waugh and self-styled 'Bishop of the Medway' Roger Gleaves, notorious homosexualist and paedophile. Are they related by any chance?*

Yours sincerely,
ENA COURTAULD (Mrs),
Whirlpool Farm, Burwash, Sussex.

Sticks almost everything around the home.

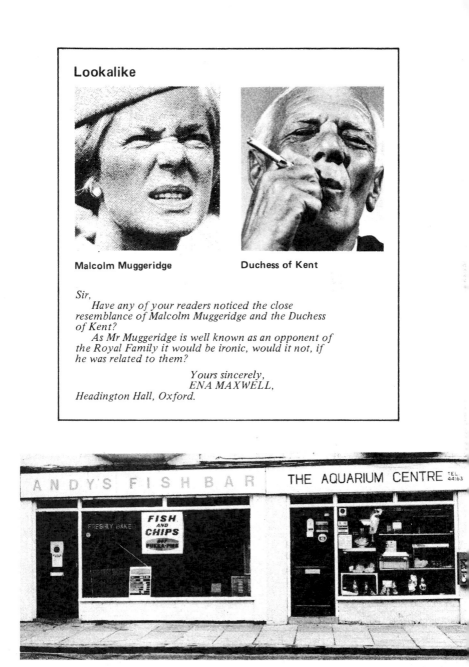

Lookalike

Malcolm Muggeridge

Duchess of Kent

Sir,
Have any of your readers noticed the close resemblance of Malcolm Muggeridge and the Duchess of Kent?
As Mr Muggeridge is well known as an opponent of the Royal Family it would be ironic, would it not, if he was related to them?

Yours sincerely,
ENA MAXWELL,
Headington Hall, Oxford.

Lookalike

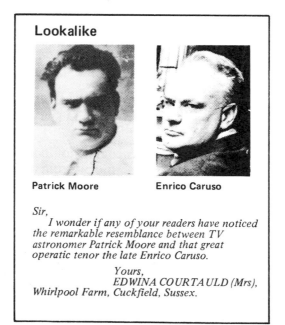

Patrick Moore

Enrico Caruso

Sir,
 I wonder if any of your readers have noticed the remarkable resemblance between TV astronomer Patrick Moore and that great operatic tenor the late Enrico Caruso.

 Yours,
 EDWINA COURTAULD (Mrs),
Whirlpool Farm, Cuckfield, Sussex.

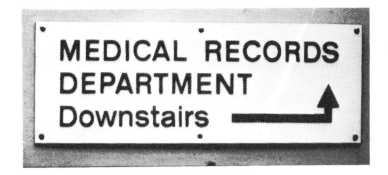

Lookalike

Descartes

Parkinson

Sir,
　　I wonder if other readers have
noticed – as I have – the likeness
between Rene Descartes and
Michael Parkinson, of 'wheelie'
fame?
　　Both well-known philosophers.
I wonder could they be in some
way related?

　　　　Yours faithfully,
　　　　P.H. HAIGH,
Shaftsbury Avenue, Timperely,
Cheshire.

HALESOWEN CATS PROTECTION LEAGUE

£1.

MICROWAVE DEMONSTRATION

Monday 21st April 8.00pm

Tickets on SALE inside

Doors Open 7.30p.m.

MODERN INDIVIDUAL ENTERPRISE
EST. 1968

Lookalike

Commodore Perry

Robert Maxwell

Sir,
    I wonder if any of your readers have noticed the extraordinary similarity between Commodore Perry, the 19th century explorer shown here in this Japanese print, and Mr Robert Maxwell, the famous newspaper owner and entrepreneur? I wonder if, by any chance, they are related?

Yours sincerely,
KEITH MILLER,
Allanton Grove, Wishaw, Lanarkshire.

Lookalike

Pint

The Maharishi

Sir,
I have recently noticed that our dog, Pint, bears a striking resemblance to His Holiness The Maharishi Mahesh Yogi.
Could they possibly be related?

Yours faithfully,
SEAN FOSTER,
Greenvale Road, Eltham, London SE9.

Lookalike

Clement Freud

Edward VII

Sir,
*   I wonder how many of your readers have noted as I have the close resemblance between the young Prince of Wales (later Edward VII) and Mr Clement Freud? Does the latter perhaps, have Royal blood in his veins?*

*   Yours sincerely,*
*   ENA COURTAULD (Mrs)*
Whirlpool Farm, Etchingham, Sussex.

This Shop is Closed all Week unless Open. Please, don't waste your time by waiting.

Lonesome Depot →

South London Crematorium ►

Lookalike

The Princess

The General

Sir,
I wonder if any of your readers have noticed the remarkable and suspicious resemblance between General Menendez of Argentina and Her Royal Highness Princess Anne. Were our brave boys being duped into going to the Falkland Islands? Has there been a top level coverup?
We should be told!

Yours faithfully,
EDITH CLAVITT,
Rose Cottage, Cobbaton, Devonshire.

Lookalike

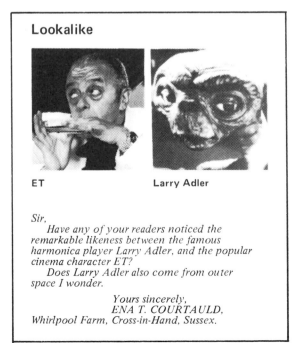

ET   Larry Adler

Sir,
Have any of your readers noticed the
remarkable likeness between the famous
harmonica player Larry Adler, and the popular
cinema character ET?
Does Larry Adler also come from outer
space I wonder.

Yours sincerely,
ENA T. COURTAULD,
Whirlpool Farm, Cross-in-Hand, Sussex.

Lookalike

Frankie Howerd **President Brezhnev**

Sir,
 I wonder if any of your readers have noticed the startling resemblance between the late President Brezhnev of the USSR and Frankie Howerd. Are they perchance related? I think we should be told.

 Yours sincerely,
 NIGEL CHING,
The Old Friendship, Eastgate,
Cawston, Norfolk.

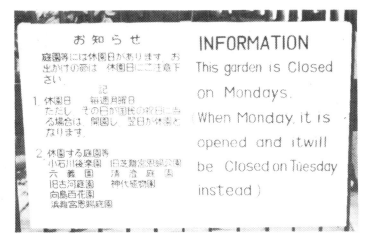

お知らせ

庭園等には休園日があります。お出かけの前は、休園日にご注意下さい。

記

1. 休園日　毎週月曜日
   ただし、その日が国民の祝日に当る場合は、開園し、翌日が休園となります。

2. 休園する庭園等
   小石川後楽園　旧芝離宮恩賜庭園
   六　義　園　　清　澄　庭　園
   旧古河庭園　　神代植物園
   向島百花園
   浜離宮恩賜庭園

INFORMATION

This garden is Closed on Mondays.

When Monday, it is opened and it will be Closed on Tuesday instead)

Lookalike

Walter Bailey

Arthur Scargill

Sir,
Have any of your readers noticed the resemblance between miners' leader Arthur Scargill and American folk-singer Walter Bailey from Nashville, Tennessee? I wonder if they are by any chance related?

Yours sincerely,
ENA B. MAXWELL,

Headington, Oxford.

Lookalike

Dubuffet

Lord Longford

Sir,
    On a recent visit to the Pompidou Centre in Paris my eye was caught by a portrait by Jean Dubuffet which bore a marked resemblance to the well known prison visitor and publisher of Lace, *Lord Longford. I wonder if he and the sitter are related.*

    Yours sincerely,
    ENA MAXWELL,
Headington Hall, Oxford.

Lookalike

George Michael

Desperate Dan

Sir,
*   I wonder if some of your readers have noticed the resemblance between George Michael and Desperate Dan? Are they by any chance related? Wasn't George Michael once related to Diana, Princess of Wales?*

*   Yours faithfully,*
*   J. GRADWELL,*
Lostick, Bolton.

God's promise:

Call upon
Me
in the day
of trouble;
I will
deliver
you

Psalm 50:15

"Make someone happy
with a phone call"

Seek ye
the LORD
while He may
be found
call ye upon Him
while He is
near Isaiah 55.6

F. S.
SPLINKLER INLET
消防
花洒入水製
快達消防公司

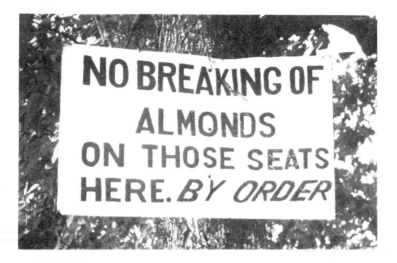

Lookalike

Anthony Howard

Dr Milton Obote

Sir,

I wonder if any of your readers have noted the close resemblance between Mr Anthony Howard deputy editor of the Observer, *and Dr Milton Obote, formerly leader of Uganda?*

Both are men known for their left-wing views. I wonder if by any chance they are related?

Yours,
ENA COURTAULD,
Whirlpool Farm, Hadlow Down, Sussex.

Lookalike

Simone de Beauvoir   **Hilda Ogden**

Sir,
    I wonder if any of your readers have been struck as I have by the similarity between Simone de Beauvoir, author of The Second Sex, *and Jean Alexander (alias* Coronation Street *character Hilda Ogden).*
    I wonder if they are by any chance related and think that we should be told.

        Yours perplexed,
        BRYAN J. MASON,
Newnham Road, London N22.

CLOSED
ON ACCOUNT OF
THE WEATHER
PLEASE COME IN

Lookalike

Eva Braun   **Margaret Thatcher**

Sir,
*   Have any of your readers noticed, as I have,*
the remarkable resemblance between Mrs
Thatcher and the late Eva Braun?
*   I wonder if by any chance they were*
related?

*   Mrs ENA COURTAULD,*
Whirlpool Farm, Kintbury, Berks.

Lookalike

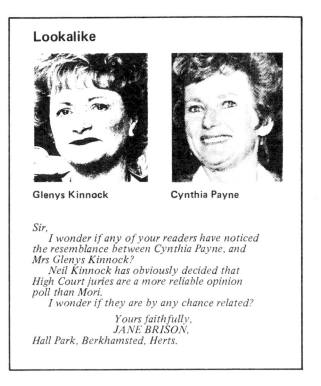

Glenys Kinnock

Cynthia Payne

Sir,
 I wonder if any of your readers have noticed the resemblance between Cynthia Payne, and Mrs Glenys Kinnock?
 Neil Kinnock has obviously decided that High Court juries are a more reliable opinion poll than Mori.
 I wonder if they are by any chance related?

   Yours faithfully,
   JANE BRISON,
Hall Park, Berkhamsted, Herts.

The entrance is forbidden to children under 4 years

Members of the audience are kindly asked not to take:

- ■ any glassware
- ■ any portable refrigerators
- ■ any encumbering objects
- ■ any dogs

into the Arena

Lookalike

Vincent Van Gogh

Nigel Pratt-Dumpster

Sir,
    I wonder if any of your readers have noticed the resemblance between the post-impressionist painter Vincent Van Gogh and the former greatest living Englishman, Nigel Pratt-Dumpster? I wonder if by any chance they are related?
    I wonder if Mr Pratt-Dumpster is deficient in an organ by self-mutilation?

Yours faithfully,
TONY GOODALL,
Dover Mansions, Canterbury Crescent, London SW9.

Lookalike

Prince Charles

Woody Allen

Sir,
    Woody Allen and Prince Charles are both known for their zany humour and slightly skewed view of the universe but are they by any chance related?

                    Sincerely,
                    STEVE TURNER,
Cromwell Road, London SW7

ookalike

amuel Beckett   A.N. Eagle

Sir,
  I wonder if any of your readers have noticed the similarity between Samuel Beckett and A.N. Eagle. Are they by any chance related?

  ENA B. HOROVITZ,
  Little-Boggis-in-the-Wold, Salop.

Lookalike

Sir Laurens van der Post

Bobby Charlton

Sir,
Have any of your readers noticed the remarkable resemblance between Mrs Thatcher's adviser Sir Laurens van der Post and the former England football captain Bobbie Charlton?
I wonder if they are by any chance related.

Yours sincerely,
ENA MAXWELL,
Headington Hall, Oxford.

Lookalike

Clive Sinclair

Clive Sinclair

Sir,
I wonder whether any of your readers have noticed the extraordinary resemblance between Sir Clive Sinclair, the inventor of popular computers, and Clive Sinclair, the author of the *Jewish Chronicle*? The glasses seem to me rather an amateur attempt at disguise.

Yours faithfully,
CHRISTOPHER HAWTREE,
Albert Palace Mansions, Lurline Gardens, London.

SWINDELLS AND GENTRY

CHARTERED ACCOUNTANTS

-1026A-

SIELSIEKES EN
NIE-BLANKE HUWELIKE

MENTAL PATIENTS AND
NON-WHITE MARRIAGES

HOURS
MONDAY to FRIDAY   8.30-1, 1.45-3

URE
MAANDAG tot VRYDAG   8.30-1, 1.45-3

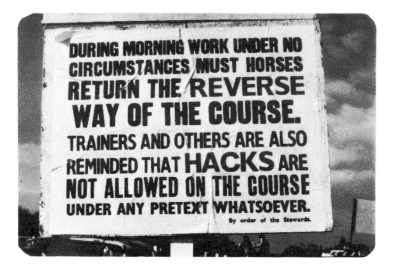

DURING MORNING WORK UNDER NO CIRCUMSTANCES MUST HORSES RETURN THE REVERSE WAY OF THE COURSE. TRAINERS AND OTHERS ARE ALSO REMINDED THAT **HACKS** ARE NOT ALLOWED ON THE COURSE UNDER ANY PRETEXT WHATSOEVER.

By order of the Stewards.

Lookalike

Scargill

Rossini

Sir,
I wonder if any of your readers have noticed the curious similarity between Rossini, King of Opera and Scargill, King Arthur of the Coalfields?

JOHNNY MADGE,
Maypole Cottage, Soberton, Southampton.

FIRE ESCAPE STAIR
DANGER-KEEP OFF

Toilets

LADIES

HAVE YOU
PAID AND
DISPLAYED ?

Lookalike

Bishop Tutu   **Larry Adler**

Sir,
*   Have any of your readers noticed the*
remarkable similarity between Larry Adler,
the famous letter writer and Bishop Desmond
Tutu?
*   I wonder if by any chance they are related?*

*   Yours sincerely,*
*   ENA B. MAXWELL,*
Headington Hall, Oxon.

Lookalike

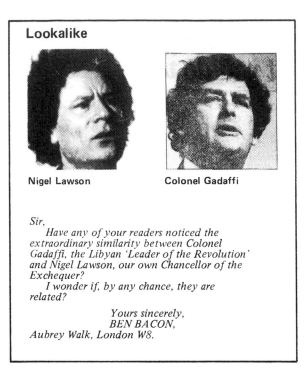

Nigel Lawson   Colonel Gadaffi

Sir,
    Have any of your readers noticed the extraordinary similarity between Colonel Gadaffi, the Libyan 'Leader of the Revolution' and Nigel Lawson, our own Chancellor of the Exchequer?
    I wonder if, by any chance, they are related?

    Yours sincerely,
    BEN BACON,
Aubrey Walk, London W8.

Lookalike

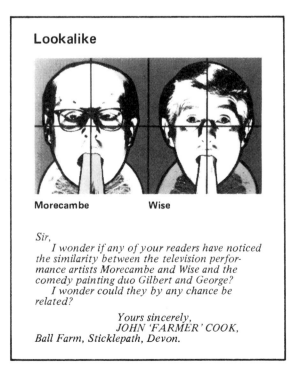

Morecambe   **Wise**

Sir,
    I wonder if any of your readers have noticed the similarity between the television performance artists Morecambe and Wise and the comedy painting duo Gilbert and George?
    I wonder could they by any chance be related?

        Yours sincerely,
        JOHN 'FARMER' COOK,
Ball Farm, Sticklepath, Devon.

Lookalike

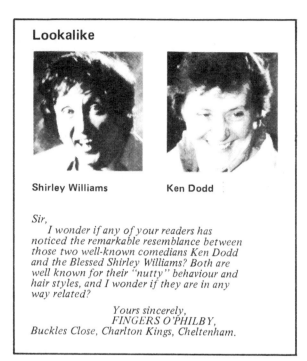

Shirley Williams   **Ken Dodd**

Sir,
  I wonder if any of your readers has noticed the remarkable resemblance between those two well-known comedians Ken Dodd and the Blessed Shirley Williams? Both are well known for their "nutty" behaviour and hair styles, and I wonder if they are in any way related?

Yours sincerely,
FINGERS O'PHILBY,
Buckles Close, Charlton Kings, Cheltenham.

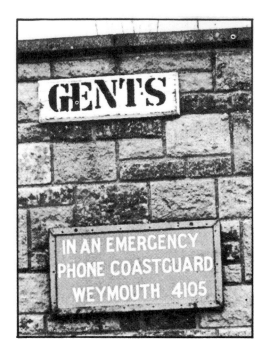

Lookalike

Sun Yun-suan   **Lord Clark**

Sir,
Have any of your readers noticed the
remarkable resemblance between the late Lord
Clark (of BBC Civilisation *fame) and Mr Sun*
Yun-suan, Prime Minister of Taiwan?
I wonder if they are by any chance related?

Yours sincerely,
ENA COURTAULD,
McTavish Farm, Auchtermuchty.

Lookalike

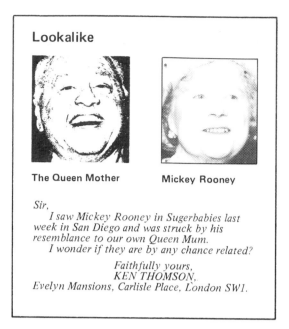

The Queen Mother

Mickey Rooney

Sir,
I saw Mickey Rooney in Sugerbabies last
week in San Diego and was struck by his
resemblance to our own Queen Mum.
I wonder if they are by any chance related?

Faithfully yours,
KEN THOMSON,
Evelyn Mansions, Carlisle Place, London SW1.

Site for new Kingdom Hall
of JEHOVAH'S WITNESSES
to be erected in two days

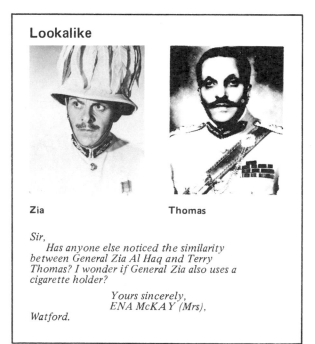

Lookalike

Zia

Thomas

Sir,
   Has anyone else noticed the similarity
between General Zia Al Haq and Terry
Thomas? I wonder if General Zia also uses a
cigarette holder?

          Yours sincerely,
          ENA McKAY (Mrs),
Watford.

Lookalike

Mick Jagger

Anita Loos

Sir,
    Has any other reader noticed the strong resemblance of Mick Jagger and the late Anita Loos?
    I wonder if by any chance they were related?

    Yours faithfully,
    CHRISTOPHER MARSDEN,
The Dene, Kirkburton, Huddersfield, West Yorks.

Lookalike

Andy   Fergie

Sir,
  Have any of your readers noticed the similarity between Les Dawson and his girlfriend Tracey Roper, and the Duke and Duchess of York?
  I wonder if by any chance they are related? If so, I think we should be told.

Yours sincerely,
ENA B. MAXWELL,
Headington Hall, Headington, Oxon.

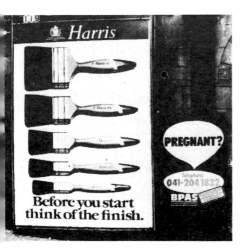

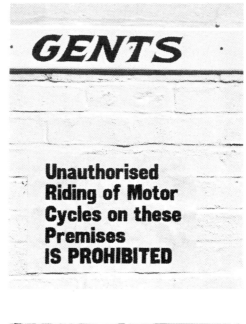

Unauthorised Riding of Motor Cycles on these Premises IS PROHIBITED

Lookalike

James Anderton   **Robert de Niro**

Sir,
    Have any of your readers noticed the
resemblance between James Anderton, Chief
Constable of Greater Manchester and Robert
('The Mission') de Niro? I wonder if by any
chance they are related?

    Yours truly,
    KATE KNOWLES,
Wallingford Avenue, London W10.

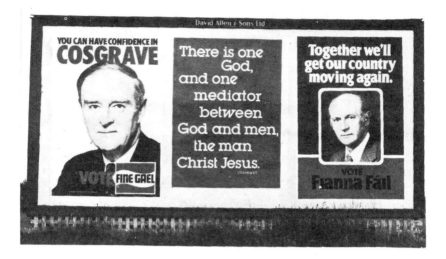

CHERRETTS

FUNERAL DIRECTORS
&
CARPET SHOWROOM

Lookalike

Margaret Thatcher   **Gargoyle**

Sir,
  I recently noticed the remarkable resemblance of a gargoyle at Dorchester Abbey, Oxon, to our beloved Prime Minister. I wonder if they are by any chance related?

  Yours sincerely,
  ENA T. MAXWELL,
C/o The Daily Mirror, Holborn, London.

Lookalike

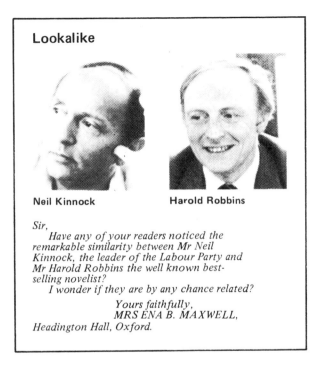

Neil Kinnock   **Harold Robbins**

Sir,
Have any of your readers noticed the remarkable similarity between Mr Neil Kinnock, the leader of the Labour Party and Mr Harold Robbins the well known best-selling novelist?
I wonder if they are by any chance related?

Yours faithfully,
MRS ENA B. MAXWELL,
Headington Hall, Oxford.

Lookalike

Alfred Brendel　　　　　Ian McCaskill

Sir,
　Have any of your readers noticed the extra-ordinary similarity between the famous pianist, Alfred Brendel and the BBC weatherman Ian McCaskill?
　I wonder if they are by any chance related?

Yours sincerely,
ENA B. MAXWELL,
Headington Hall, Oxon.

Lookalike

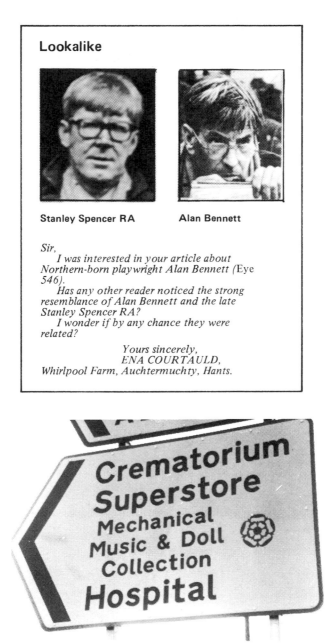

Stanley Spencer RA   **Alan Bennett**

Sir,
    I was interested in your article about Northern-born playwright Alan Bennett (Eye 546).
    Has any other reader noticed the strong resemblance of Alan Bennett and the late Stanley Spencer RA?
    I wonder if by any chance they were related?

Yours sincerely,
ENA COURTAULD,
Whirlpool Farm, Auchtermuchty, Hants.

Crematorium Superstore
Mechanical Music & Doll Collection
Hospital

Lookalike

Michael Heseltine

Kirk Douglas

Sir,
    I wonder if any other readers have noted as I have the close resemblance of Mr Michael Heseltine and Hollywood actor Kirk Douglas.
    Are they by any chance related?

    Yours sincerely,
    ETHEL MARNHAM (Mrs),
'Arafat', Abergavenny, Gwent.

Lookalike

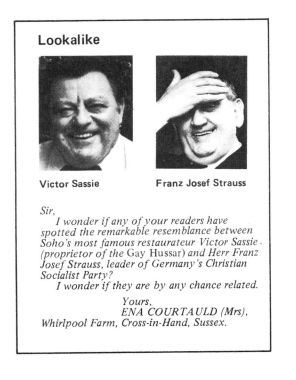

Victor Sassie   **Franz Josef Strauss**

Sir,
I wonder if any of your readers have
spotted the remarkable resemblance between
Soho's most famous restaurateur Victor Sassie
(proprietor of the Gay Hussar) *and Herr Franz*
Josef Strauss, leader of Germany's Christian
Socialist Party?
I wonder if they are by any chance related.

Yours,
ENA COURTAULD (Mrs),
Whirlpool Farm, Cross-in-Hand, Sussex.

Lookalike

Sir,

    Have any of your readers noticed the similarity between the newly discovered manuscript of Franz Liszt and the works of L.S. Lowry? I wonder if by any chance they are related?

        Yours sincerely,
        MALCOLM KNOTT,
Temple, London EC4.

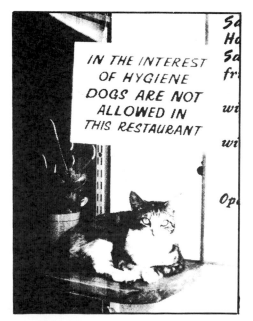

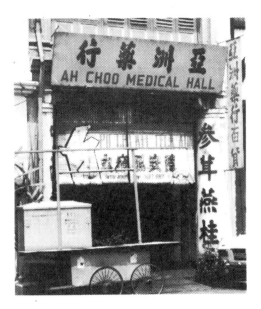

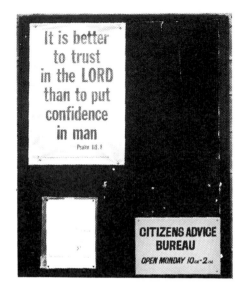

Lookalike

Freddie Mercury   **Lord Lucan**

Sir,
*   It can now be exclusively revealed that Lord Lucan is not missing and has actually been living in the UK all the time. Other people have been foiled into thinking that he is really called Freddie Mercury.*
*   Or am I wrong? They may just be brothers — Lord Mercury or Freddie Lucan. I think we should be told.*

*   Yours about-to-instigate-a-public-inquiryly.*
*   Mr S. WILLIAMSON,*
Lon Pobty, Bangor, Gwynedd.

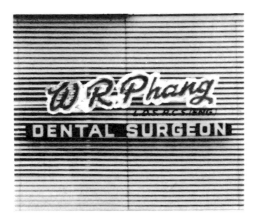

Non-Lookalike

Bob Hoskins   Bob Hoskins

Sir,
   Have any of your readers noticed the extra-ordinary lack of similarity between the actor Bob Hoskins and the new model of Bob Hoskins in Madame Tussauds?
   Are they by any chance related?

              Yours sincerely,
              ENA B. HARTLEY.

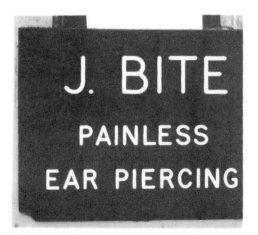

LEECH'S
FUNERAL SERVICE

Get down under 3 hours quicker.

British
airways

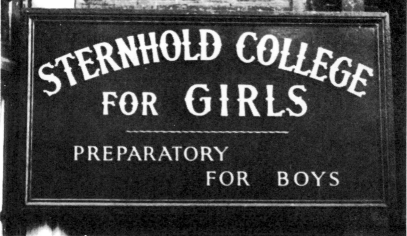

STERNHOLD COLLEGE
FOR GIRLS

PREPARATORY
FOR BOYS

Lookalike

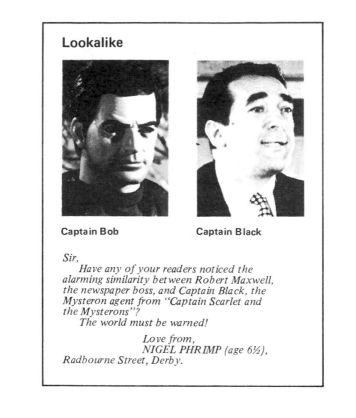

Captain Bob   **Captain Black**

Sir,
    Have any of your readers noticed the
alarming similarity between Robert Maxwell,
the newspaper boss, and Captain Black, the
Mysteron agent from "Captain Scarlet and
the Mysterons"?
    The world must be warned!

       Love from,
       NIGEL PHRIMP (age 6½),
Radbourne Street, Derby.

Lookalike

Harvey-Jones

Balzac

Sir,
I wonder if any of your readers have noticed the extraordinary similarity between Sir John Harvey-Jones, the ex-chairman of ICI, and Honore de Balzac, the well-known French novelist.
Are they by any chance related?

Yours faithfully,
ENA B. MAXWELL,
Headington, Oxford.

FEMALE DRESSING & SPECTATORS →

Lookalike

Mr David Bowie

Dr David Owen

Sir,
Have any of your readers noticed the
uncanny resemblance between Dr David Owen,
leader of the SDP, and David Bowie, the
popular singer?
I wonder if by any chance they are related?

Yours sincerely,
ENA T. MAXWELL,
Headington Hall, Oxford.

Lookalike

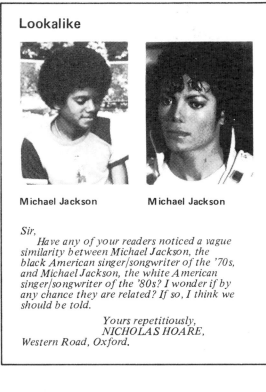

Michael Jackson   Michael Jackson

Sir,
   *Have any of your readers noticed a vague
similarity between Michael Jackson, the
black American singer/songwriter of the '70s,
and Michael Jackson, the white American
singer/songwriter of the '80s? I wonder if by
any chance they are related? If so, I think we
should be told.*

               Yours repetitiously,
               NICHOLAS HOARE,
Western Road, Oxford.

Lookalike

Prince Andrew   **Prince Edward**

Sir,

Have any of your readers noticed the extraordinary resemblance between Prince Andrew and his brother Prince Edward?

I wonder if they are by any chance related?

Yours faithfully,
ENA T. MAXWELL,
Headington Hall, Oxford.